The 1 packer guide
Globetrotting on bare essentials

Renata Lanzoni

Published by Renata Lanzoni
First Edition
ISBN: 9781686187117
Copyright © Renata Lanzoni 2019 – All rights reserved

Renata Lanzoni has asserted her right under the Copyright, Designs and Patents Act 1988 to be identified as the author of this work.

All rights reserved. No part of this publication may be reproduced, stored in a retrieval system, or transmitted in any form or by any means, electronic, mechanical, photocopying, recording or otherwise, without the prior permission of the copyright owner.

Printed in Great Britain
by Amazon

THE LIGHT-PACKER GUIDE

HAPPY AND SAFE LIGHT TRAVELS!

- Adaptor
- Sunglasses
- Small combination padlock
- Clear plastic food bag
- Earphones
- Earplugs
- Tweezers
- Nail clippers
- Nail file
- Lip balm
- Toothbrush
- Small tube of toothpaste
- Nausea bracelets
- Roll-on deodorant
- Shampoo/conditioner bar
- Comb/brush
- Hair ties
- Pain relief tablets
- A few plasters

List for men

- Passport/National ID
- Driving licence
- Credit cards
- Smartphone
- Smartphone charger
- Sim pin
- Earphones
- Earplugs
- Pen
- Reusable straw
- 1 zip up lightweight hoodie
- 4 T-shirts/tank tops
- 4 shorts
- 1 long light trousers
- 1 flip-flops
- 1 "flip-flops socks"
- 1 warm socks
- 2 underwear
- 1 swimming trunk
- 1 pyjama
- 1 large microfiber towel
- 1 Sarong
- Small fabric day bag/drawstring
- Pack-away backpack/bag
- Photocopy of passport and driving licence
- 4 or more passport photographs
- Battery pack
- 2 small money purses
- Glasses/contact lenses
- Collapsible reusable water bottle

- Battery pack
- 2 small money purses
- Glasses/contact lenses
- Collapsible reusable water bottle
- Adaptor
- Sunglasses
- Small combination padlock
- Clear plastic food bag
- Earphones
- Earplugs
- Tweezers
- Nail clippers
- Nail file
- Lip balm
- Toothbrush
- Small tube of toothpaste
- Nausea bracelets
- Roll-on deodorant
- Shampoo/conditioner bar
- Comb/brush
- Hair ties
- Pain relief tablets
- A few plaster

List for women

- Passport/National ID
- Driving licence
- Credit cards
- Smartphone
- Smartphone charger
- Sim pin
- Earphones
- Earplugs
- Pen
- Reusable straw
- 1 zip up lightweight hoodie
- 4 T-shirts/vest tops
- 2 skirts
- 2 dresses
- 1 shorts
- 1 leggings or long, light trousers
- 1 flip-flops
- 1 "flip-flops socks"
- 1 warm socks
- 2 underwear
- 1 brasseries
- 1 very light wrap top
- 1 swimsuit
- 1 pyjama
- 1 large microfiber towel
- 1 Sarong
- Small fabric day bag/drawstring
- Pack-away backpack/bag
- Photocopy of passport and driving licence
- 4 or more passport photographs

THE LIST

Until you are a super sharp light-packer and have mastered the art of taking only the indispensable, I would recommend making a list of everything you take with you and update it with anything you had to buy during your travels. Once you get home, analyse this list to see what you have used and what you just carried around with you. This information will be invaluable for your next travel.

You can print the following list of my bare essentials and add to it any items you decide to bring over and above the existing list and any item you buy on the road. You can indeed delete any of the items I deem essential if you do not share my opinion.

Exercise

If you are a keen sportsperson, I hope you know you can exercise pretty much every muscle without the need for any machinery or various tools and weights. If travelling around is not exercise enough for you, you can build a small daily routine and do your push-ups, press-ups, squats, lunges and abs pretty much anywhere. Jogging is a cost-free sport and does not add to your luggage. Of course, I would suggest you take precaution if you want to do this in tropical temperatures. The point is that you do not need to bring anything specific with you on your travels to ensure you give your body a regular work out.

Please remember that these are just my tips based on my experience and that your items need to serve you. Bring what makes you feel happy and safe but always be mindful that things are not experiences and things weight you down. Don't be afraid of shedding luggage that does not serve you while you are on the road, someone else will be very grateful to be able to use your items.
I wish you a lot of amazing experiences visiting this beautiful world we live in.

example, that travel guitars sound very good and are a lot more transportable than the original-sized one. But if you really cannot part with yours for a few weeks or months, you will need to find a way to bring it with you. Please consider the advantages and disadvantages of your decision carefully.

Make-up

Makeup is not generally something you will need to bring with you on a backpacking trip. The heat will make it run, and the sun will give you a much better glow than any product you can buy. If you can't think of parting with all your makeup, I would suggest you just bring some eyeliner, mascara and lip colour.

Laundry

You find cheap and quick laundry places pretty much everywhere in the world. However, I would recommend you buy a small sachet of washing powder (unless you have a shampoo bar, which can be used for laundry) and wash your small items daily, leaving to dry overnight. You will find that it only takes you a few minutes to do this, and you will avoid running out of clean clothes and filling your bag with smelly items.

Jewellery

I would strongly recommend not to bring any high-value jewellery or anything that has an important sentimental value to you. There are several reasons for this. On the one hand, you will be travelling and will have these items with you from the moment you set off from home to the day you get back. You will be responsible for them wherever you are, and you might not be able to guarantee they will not get lost or stolen. This is a worry you might want to avoid. On the other hand, some of the countries you visit might be a lot more disadvantaged than yours. I believe that flaunting an item of jewellery in front of people who are in difficulty is not the most emphatic thing to do.

Musical instruments

Many backpackers are brilliant musicians. Because of this, many of the people you encounter in your travels carry their own instruments and are very happy to let you play them. You do not really need to bring yours. As an alternative, I have also seen travellers borrowing instruments from music shops for the duration of their stay in that particular place. However, if you really cannot conceive living without your instrument, investigate investing in a travel version of it. I know, for

If you find it is really too sunny for you to cope and you need to be in the sun at peak times, try to do what the locals do and buy a small umbrella instead. It is less damaging for your health and you can always use it in downpours, too.

Tools

If you intend to carry out a trade and need tools for it, you will have to make sure your backpack has enough room for all of them. I met a person who was travelling with a massive backpack full of his juggling and trick gear which he collected on the road but never really used. If you are making a living out of your trade, the extra weight is justifiable, but if you are carrying it around hoping to one day maybe use these tools, you are not being kind to your back. The question is: do you need them? Can you find them when you want to use them without carrying them around all the time?

Shaving

Shaving creams for both men and women can be found pretty much everywhere, as can razors and ultimately even barbers and beauty salons. You certainly do not need to stock up before leaving.

nice memento pictures, invest in a good smartphone with a decent camera and just take that. Unless the quality of your snaps is absolutely crucial for your livelihood, I would not lug around a professional camera.

Mosquito repellent

This is not necessary in every country you visit. I would try a day or two without it and see if it is possible to avoid smothering yourself in it. I have also found that coconut oil helps guard against mosquito bites. Unless you are in the jungle or in very green areas, mosquitos seem to be active only for a short time at sunrise and sunset. You might be able to cover up with long trousers or sleeves just for those times and not need any repellent.

However, if your destination is at risk of malaria, then take the necessary precautions.

Sun-cream

I am not too keen on sun cream for the sake of using it. I think you are much better off staying away from direct sunlight when it is at its peak and tan gradually. Cover up and limit exposure rather than plaster chemicals on your skin.

probably post from a good smartphone if they are not too ambitious.

Most of the countries have Internet cafes or internet points where you can access a normal computer if your smartphone is not enough for you.

Just remember to save all your important documents on the Cloud somewhere so you can access them from anywhere with any device you choose and will not lose them should your device be lost or stolen.

If a laptop is your only answer, then please investigate if you can purchase the lightest possible version that still has every feature you will possibly need. Remember to pack laptops and/or tablets flush against your back. There is usually a tight compartment to the back of your backpack. Using this will make the weight of your computer a lot easier to carry. And whatever you decide to bring, whether it is a laptop or a table, make sure you remember to pack the charger, too!

Professional cameras

Ask yourself if you are such a professional photographer that you really need to carry with you the valuable and heavy special camera you have at home. If photography is your job, I can't argue with that, but if you want to take the paper volumes with you. Or alternatively, do your research before you leave home and take pictures of the pages of the guide that really interest you.

Maps

As with guide books, I would not bring any paper map with me. Google Maps are excellent most of the times, and My Map is brilliant if there is no Internet connection. Just download the app and the maps of the places you need.

Failing that, I have always found that asking people for directions is an easy and fun way to find your way and get to know the local culture.

Laptops

I have met many people who logged laptops with them and had probably used them a couple of times in months. I wouldn't carry one. It is heavy, it is valuable and impacts your security considerations. If you work on a laptop at home and you are definitely sure you cannot do your job using just a smartphone, then investigate tablets. They are a lot lighter. Unless your job involves specific programs and complicated designs, you will probably be able to carry it out using a smaller device. Bloggers can around, but I know some of you might have a different opinion.

Books

I am an avid reader and love the feel of a real book however, for the sake of my back, I can easily do without the paperbacks during my travels. If you like reading, download an app and some e-books on your phone, and you can read away without extra weight. This is also incredibly practical as it allows you to read at night without the need to have a light on.

Also remember that you can "borrow" books from most hostels and guest-houses around the world, read them and leave them at your next destination. This is a great way of passing on culture and saving trees.

Guide books

I would not carry guide books as they are very heavy and if you are travelling for a few months you would need to bring a lot of them to cover all the countries in your itinerary. We are lucky to live in an era where everything can be found online, so I would just research on the Internet the places I want to visit. If some specific guide books are essential for you, then buy the e-book versions and have them at your fingertips without having to carry

Small combination padlock

Generally, hostels provide lockers, but you usually have to supply your own lock. If a locker is not provided and you feel your things are not safe, you can also use the lock to secure the zipper of your backpack shut, by locking the end bits together. A combination lock is more practical than a standard one, as there is no key that can get lost, and you can share the combination with a fellow traveller if you need to.

Denim

Unless absolutely necessary and you cannot leave without your jeans, I would strongly advise against packing them. They are heavy, generally tight-fitting, difficult to wash and take a long time to dry. A good pair of cotton trousers or leggings are a lot more practical all around.

Neck pillow

Use a folded hoodie/sarong or towel or bring an inflatable pillow that folds down to nothing. Normal neck pillows are bulky and get grimy being carried around on the outside of your backpack or use valuable space in the inside. The amount of time you will actually use a neck pillow does not usually warrant carrying it

bottles of water a day is irresponsible. There is no excuse these days for not reducing our carbon footprint if we can. There are innovative collapsible water bottles which can be packed away in your backpack and refilled during your journey. Many places these days have refill stations, and I have found that hostels throughout the world are particularly good with having free or very cheap water refill fountains that offer safe, filtered water.

There is a wide variety of collapsible reusable bottles on the market and you need to find the one that suits your requirements. They are much better than hard bottles for us travellers, as they take up very little space when empty, and are flexible, easier to carry if full and weight very little. I would suggest opting for two 500 ml bottles. In doing so, I have the flexibility of carrying 500 ml for a shorter trip or 1 litre split into two bottles. Much more flexible all around.

Alternatively, you can go a step further and invest in a water filtration system bottle. Yes, that means bringing it from home and therefore adding to your luggage, which goes against my creed, but in this case, I feel it is totally justified. You can then re-fill this pretty much anywhere and drink clean filtered water wherever you are. There are collapsible versions of this on the market, too.

not be allowed to bring your liquids in your hand luggage.

Earphones

I would not bring any bulky headphones that take up a lot of space in your pack and are more vulnerable. I have found that a set of small, practical earbuds are more than enough.

Personal reusable straws

Our main aim, when we travel, is to stay safe AND to minimise our impact on the environment while learning about our beautiful world. Plastic straws are unfortunately still widely used, but it doesn't mean you have to use them. While you do not want to use plastic, you certainly do not want to put your mouth on the rim of bottles that could be contaminated. Invest in a metal or bamboo straw, and bring it with you everywhere you go.

Collapsible reusable water bottle

Water is sold everywhere, and it is generally cheap. However, I would suggest that a savvy traveller could do a lot for the environment. Although water is available, the amount of plastic litter we produce by buying several dries within one hour – guys, this is your essential piece of gear, too.

Small day bag

This is very useful to store all your essentials while travelling and to carry what you need on a tour or a day trip. Put everything in it that is in your pockets when travelling through airports, so you can be quick at security.

Pack away backpack/bag

This can be used as laundry bag, bag for longer excursions, beach bag or for any souvenirs you pick up on your trip. It can be folded very small when not in use and it usually weights only a few grams.

Liquids

Do not carry liquids if possible, as they might spill and make a mess of your backpack. If you do, make sure they are well sealed in plastic bags and away from any electronic equipment. Most airports require you to show liquids separately when going through security, and you are not allowed to bring containers bigger than 100 ml. Make sure you stay below the requirements or you will

Flip-flop socks

These are socks I have found in Asia and have a split between the big toe and the other toes so you can wear them with flip flops. As an alternative, look for socks with toes, which are sold pretty much anywhere. With these socks you do away with the need for closed-toed shoes and socks to travel with, as you can wear your flip-flops and still keep your feet warm.

Pyjama

I tend to use a vest top and very light trousers to sleep in. Although you might not use anything to sleep in while at home in hot temperatures, remember you are likely to share dorms, so you need some decency.

Sarong/Pareo

This is my multi-task friend and it will be yours too, trust me. Ladies can use it as a skirt or dress. You can take it with you when visiting places of worship if what you are wearing does not cover you enough. It functions as a bottom sheet, if where you are staying is a bit grubby, or a top sheet for a bit of extra warmth. It can be wrapped around the shoulders if it gets cold, and you can use it to lay on at the beach. It is very light, can be washed and

should you run short. Of course, if you are not comfortable with a bikini, or if you are planning on some serious diving and need an all-in one swimsuit, pack two bras (unless you are OK letting the girls loose under a T-shirt while your bra is drying).

For the boys, swimming trunks double up as shorts, giving you more options of wardrobe, and I dare say are more comfortable than tight swimming gear.

Skirts

I favour wrap arounds lightweight cotton skirts that go below the knees. In most places of worship, you need to be covered to below the knees, so these are perfect to avoid extra charges or disappointment. You can use these skirts to lie on the beach, avoiding the need to bring a beach towel or sarong. You can also use your skirt as an extra cover during cold nights.

Shorts

For both boys and girls, I would advise to bring light weight, comfortable shorts. For boys, if one of the pairs of shorts in your luggage can be unfolded to just below the knee, you will not have problems in places of worship (see above about skirts).

that you cannot lose your unique writing, nobody can read it without your permission, and you do not have to carry extra weight.

Torch

I have never carried a torch with me. These days, all smart phones have a torchlight, so I would just use that. This means, however, that you have to be consistent and disciplined at charging your smartphone (and your battery pack) on a regular basis. Some countries suffer from power cuts and extensive blackouts. While a few hours is not necessarily a problem, a few days might be. So if you know your destination is likely to be problematic, bring a small torch. Generally, blackouts are not usually as bad as they sound and unless you plan on long hikes in the jungle at night, I really do not think a torch is a necessary item to bring.

Swimwear

I try to use every item I bring in more than one way, so my swimwear suggestion is a bikini for the girls and swimming trunks for the boys.

Bikini tops can double up as brasserie when your trusted one is drying. The bottom can be used as underwear, flip-flops are a lot more practical than shoes in these situations.

Sandals

You can of course bring these to alternate with your flip-flops. However, in my experience, people who are wearing sandals only do so because they have brought them along. If they hadn't, they wouldn't have missed them.

Hat

A sun hat might be a good idea, especially for heads with thinning hair, but make sure it is not a large, frilly sun hat, especially not made of straw or any hard material. Much as it might be pretty, it is incredibly unpractical to carry around. You want to be able to fold your hat or hook it to your backpack, and you want to make sure you definitely will use it. Would a foulard or a bandana do? If so, opt for that. Much more versatile and easy to carry.

Diary

I am all for writing a journal, especially when you are travelling; however, rather than bringing your special diary with you, investigate using an online one. You can then write to your heart's content secure in the thought

Your normal bank is likely to block your credit and/or debit card while you are abroad (something based entirely on algorithms), and unless you spend considerable time and money calling them from wherever you are to get your card unblocked, you have problems. Without my travel card, I would have had big problems on several occasions. At one stage, my normal bank cards were blocked, so I couldn't buy flight tickets to move on to my next destination. I couldn't even call the bank, because my home sim card is topped up using my bank credit card. Yes, the one that got blocked. Thankfully, my travel credit card can be topped up by anyone with a similar card, so I asked a trusted friend to put some money on it. Moral of the story? Definitely invest in a travel top-up credit card.

Walking shoes

Pack these only if you think you are going to go on serious hikes. I have done most of mine in flip flops without problems. If you want to carry walking shoes, make sure they are not your new best pair. They might get lost or stolen, and you might decide to abandon them after you realise that you really do not need them. Also, be aware that in most public and tourist places (shops and temples) you are expected to remove your footwear, and way. Just remember to pack your charger and battery pack!

Sim Cards

I have gotten into the habit of buying a local data card as soon as I arrive in the country. I have found they are very cheap and give me the peace of mind of having Internet available wherever I am. I definitely recommend getting one. Once you leave the country, either discard the local sim, or store it in your phone case if you think you will be returning to the same place. You might find that topping up an existing sim is cheaper than buying a new one in some countries.

Credit cards

The right credit cards are the best travel companions. You do not want to carry a lot of cash with you, but you want the flexibility of having liquid money, as most of the countries you will visit will only accept cash payments. These days there are several top-up cards which offer commission-free cash withdrawals (up to a monthly limit) at good exchange rates. I would advise getting two of these cards to make the most of the commission-free monthly withdrawal allowance. Make sure it is a well-accepted one like Visa or MasterCard.

THE WHYS AND WHY NOTS

<u>Smartphone</u>

These days, smartphones cover several functions previously carried out by different appliances. We are lucky to have them, so let's make the most of them. My smartphone has two sim cards, this helps when I have a local card, as well as my home sim (which I deactivate unless I need it). I use my phone as: computer (by having local data cards I am on line as and when I need), map (whether on line or by downloading an app that gives me off-line maps – e.g. Maps.Me), book, tour guide, camera, diary, document writing, reading help (you can use an app that helps with reading if you find the writing too small, eliminating the need for reading glasses), music player, game-player, video, voice recorder and torch. Before setting off on your travels, make sure your phone has the ability to do all you want it to do. Download all you need and subscribe to everything you might need while on the road, as sometimes this is harder to do when you are abroad.

Make sure you have a good, sturdy case to protect your phone from the inevitable knocks, and you are on your

of the see-through bags in the middle. Spread them in such a way as to have the same depth at the top, middle and bottom of your backpack.
8. Lay your flip-flops next to each other face down on your bags, so that the soles do not touch them.
9. Hang your padlock to the outside of the backpack
10. Use your day bag for your essentials during travels.
11. Everything has a place and it is all accessible.

Once your backpack is zipped up, use the compression straps to secure everything in place. And you are done!

The items in the "essentials" category (A) are THE ONLY valuable things you will have and, the only ones you need to look after. Everything else is easily replaceable

By using the packing see-through bags, you can simply remove the relevant bag from the backpack to find the item you are looking for. Nothing else will be moved or unpacked. This method makes packing and unpacking easy, quick and neat. Pack like a Tetris game and be a luggage ninja. Give it a try!

How to organise your bare minimum

Use different coloured packing cubes/ bags to keep your items separate by category and easily identifiable within your backpack. I would suggest using see-through zipped bags; even better if they are compression ones. Plastic bags mean that even if it rains and your backpack gets wet, your clothes inside will not. You need one per category of clothing, so that you can just reach into your backpack, find the right bag and the right item inside it, without disturbing anything else in the pack.

I organise the kit above as follows:

1. A large see-through bag for skirts, dresses and trousers (roll them and position them next to each other in the bag)
2. A large bag for my pyjamas and sarong (nightwear)
3. A small one for socks, underwear, bras, swimsuit
4. A small one for the 'other items' (C), apart from the towel and sarong
5. A see-through zipped bag for the toiletries (D)
6. A clear food plastic bag for items bought on site (E)
7. Roll your towel and hoodie, and lie them on the left and right of your backpack, then put the rest

- Shampoo and conditioner. If you haven't found a shampoo/conditioner bar at home, buy a small bottle when you arrive. Some countries sell mono-use sachets which are excellent for travelling.
- Soap/shower gel, same as above, if you haven't got a shampoo bar.

I would not rush into buying shampoo and soap as soon as I arrive. If you are staying in hostels, you might find that there are plenty of products there for you to use that have been left behind by other travellers.

- Tweezers
- Nail clippers (you cannot carry nail scissors in your hand luggage)
- Nail file
- Lip balm (in a tube as the solid one will melt)
- Toothbrush (with head cover cap)
- Small tube of toothpaste
- Nausea bracelets (light to carry and you never know how rough that ferry ride can be)
- Roll-on deodorant
- Shampoo/conditioner bar (this serves me as shampoo, conditioner, soap, shower gel and laundry soap)
- Comb/brush
- Hair ties
- Pain relief tablets
- A few plasters (for those inevitable initial blisters)
- Packet of tissues or a little toilet paper (many countries do not use paper in the toilet, only a water spout)

E. **Buy on site when you arrive**

- Moisturising lotion. The best one I found is coconut oil –it is also the cheapest.

- Portable charger/battery packs, especially if you use your phone as camera, as this drains the battery. Just make it a habit to charge it regularly
- 2 small money purses (one for the currency of the country you are in, one for all the other currencies you are carrying around)
- Prescription glasses/contact lenses (if needed)
- Collapsible, reusable water bottles
- Adaptor (check what exactly you need, you might just get away with a European plug)
- Sunglasses (carry them in a small pouch or they will get scratched and become useless)
- Small combination padlock
- 2 clear plastic food bags (one to keep in your day-bag to store phone and documents in case of rain, the other for the liquids bought on site).

D. Toiletries etc.

A small see-through, zipped-up bag with these items is very useful. See-through, so you do not have to take everything out to find what you need; zipped up so the contents don't spill into your backpack.

*These are the items I will wear to travel, so they will not really be in my backpack, but on my body. As a general advice, wear your bulkiest and heaviest items while travelling.

In cold days, I layer my clothes and achieve the same result as having warmer clothes. For example, I would wear my leggings under my shorts and a vest under a T-shirt and the hoodie on top. I can use the sarong as a shawl too. I have never needed anything else.

C. Other Items

- 1 large microfiber towel (130x70cm) - this can be used as sheet or cover if needed
- 1 Sarong/pareo
- Small fabric day bag/drawstring bag (big enough for your money, phone, water and small essentials while on site)
- Pack-away backpack/bag for longer day trips where your day bag would not be enough
- Photocopy of passport and driving licence
- 4 or more passport photographs (for visas if needed. It will save you a lot of time queuing)

- 1 brasseries (I would favour black; also consider sports bras as they can double up as swim top or day top) *
- 1 very light wrap top (I carry this with me always. It is useful if the temperature drops a bit or if I need to cover my shoulders for temples/church visits or to protect them from the sun)
- 1 swimsuit
- 1 pyjama

For men
- 1 zip up lightweight hoodie *
- 4 T-shirt/ tank tops *
- 4 shorts
- 1 long light trousers *
- 1 flip-flops (make sure they are not new and will not give you blisters on the first day) *
- 1 "flip-flops socks" *
- 1 warm socks (for aeroplane, train, bus trips or cold nights)
- 2 underwear (wash each evening and it is dry by the morning) *
- 1 swimming trunk
- 1 pyjama

- Earplugs (essential if planning on staying in dormitories and for long, noisy journeys)
- Pen (useful for filling out landing cards and many other tricks)
- Reusable straw

B. <u>Clothes</u>

For women
- 1 zip up lightweight hoodie *
- 4 T-shirts/vest tops *
- 2 skirts
- 2 dresses (at least one to below the knee, so you can wear it when visiting places of worship)
- 1 shorts
- 1 leggings or long light trousers *
- 1 flip-flops (make sure they are not new and will not give you blisters on the first day) *
- 1 "flip-flops socks" *
- 1 warm socks (for aeroplane, train, bus trips or cold nights)
- 2 underwear (wash each evening and it is dry by the morning) *

THE BARE MINIMUM

Here is my combat list for a super-light backpack. I have actually travelled with these items for 4 months and I never felt I was missing out; on the contrary, seeing my travel mates struggle under the weight of their luggage and looking with envy at my small bag, I was quite happy not to have more than my bare minimum.

Your perfect packing list will be different from anyone else's, but you can follow these guidelines to ensure you do not go overboard with adding items to your bag. The only way to really get to your bare minimum list is to test it out and take notes on what worked and what didn't, so that next time you get closer to perfection.

A. <u>Essentials</u>

- Passport/National Identification Document
- Driving licence
- Credit cards
- Smartphone
- Smartphone charger
- Sim pin (store it in your phone case and make changing sims a lot easier than a paperclip)
- Earphones

- A chest strap: Is a nice-to-have, but it is not essential if your luggage is light.

- Load adjustor straps: Which pull the weight of the pack toward you. This helps with the aerodynamics and makes the backpack a lot easier to carry.

- A hook, strap or handle: Is good to have, in case you want to hang your trainers or washing that has not yet completely dried.

I have never had any need for a rain cover. Unless you plan on long trips on foot in the middle of no-where you will not really need it.

Now that you have your shell, let's find out what to put in it.

- Outside pockets: These are useful for your liquids, toiletries or small items. It is easier to reach your toiletries if they are packed separately from the rest of your belongings. It is also easier to remove them at the airport if you need to show your liquids and creams.

- Side-mesh pocket: This is good for your water bottle and is easily reached without having to remove your backpack from your shoulders.

- Side compression straps: To tighten your backpack when not full and to stabilize the load. One in the middle/high and one toward the bottom are ideal, so that your whole pack is compressed and not just the top. By doing this, you make sure that your things stay exactly how you pack them and do not slide down the bag. You also make sure that your backpack is more aerodynamic and fits your back better, making it easier to carry. Compression straps are also good to strap any additional footwear into.

- Waist-belt pockets: These are useful as, when you are travelling, especially on airlines that only allow one piece of hand-luggage, you can have some essentials at hand, e.g. money, phone, passport.

- Back reinforcement: To ensure that the backpack stays straight and does not bundle up into a ball around your waist. Ideally the reinforcement should be very light and well padded, so as not to hurt your back.

- Zipped inside pocket: This is extremely useful for your valuables. It is harder to get to than outside pockets, as thieves will need to get through two sets of zips before getting to your things. This is where I would store credit cards and documents that I do not need to have handy in my day bag.

- Opening zip: The wider the opening, the better. You definitely do not want a top-loading backpack, unless you enjoy emptying it out fully every time you look for something. A wide zip gives you easy access to your belonging, without having to move things around too much.

THE BACKPACK

To start your journey to a new, light packer you, the first thing you need to do is invest in your new travel companion: your backpack.

Let me tell you, this is not an area to take lightly. This is THE MOST CRUCIAL decision you will need to make. Too little room and you will leave some essentials out (although I seriously doubt it), or you will not have space for those little knick-knacks to bring home. Too big, and you will end up shoving far too much in it, just because there is room.

My suggestion? Do not exceed a 30 litres backpack. You can definitely get away with 20 or 25 litres too, if you are very good and do not plan on bringing home any souvenirs.

To make sure your trip is as easy and enjoyable as possible, ensure that you choose a backpack with the following characteristics:

- Waist belt: This will make it easier to carry your backpack, not overcharge your back and make you walk as straight as possible (as opposed to looking and feeling like a turtle).

SHOULD I PACK IT?

Follow this very simple diagram when deciding what to pack:

- Do you need it?
  - No → **DO NOT PACK IT!**
  - Yes → Are you sure?
    - No → **DO NOT PACK IT!**
    - Yes → Do you use it often?
      - No → **DO NOT PACK IT!**
      - Yes → Can you use something you have already packed instead?
        - Yes → **DO NOT PACK IT!**
        - No → Is it expensive to buy on site?
          - No → **DO NOT PACK IT!**
          - Yes → **PACK IT**

Please use the check list at the end of this guide as an aid to packing for your next trip. And remember, for every one of us light-packers, there are at least ten over-packers. You can always borrow something from them ;)

Pack your heavy things (if you have any) at the bottom of your backpack, to ensure comfort while carrying the bag.

Make sure you always pack your things in the same place in your backpack, so you do not have to fumble around to find them. You can go straight to them in no time, even in the dark. Also, try to keep together things you use at the same time, for example I keep my pyjamas, towel, toothpaste and toothbrush in the same spot/in the same zipped bag, as I generally use them together.

Use the pockets in your backpack to keep your items separate and easy to find. For example, I pack my electricals (chargers and adaptors) in a pocket and liquids in a separate pocket (with easy access at security checks).

I tend to stick to dark or white tops, as in warm climates, nice pretty colours show off your sweaty patches incredibly well. Dresses, skirts and trousers can be colourful; it does not impact your street credibility as much. I would however not advise on opting for light colours for anything to wear around your bottom. You will be on the road, sitting in public places, busses and trains and possibly doing your laundry by hand. Dark colours will be much kinder on the inevitable stains.

feeling comfortable in the heat, or on a plane, when your body bloats.

To avoid creases and to pack more efficiently, try rolling your clothes especially dresses, skirts and shirts. Fold the sides to the middle, so that your item is now 1/3 wide, then start rolling it from the top down. You can then pack your rolled items side by side, rather than having them one on top of the other. This will make it easier to see all your belongings rather than having to lift them out of the bag to find what you are looking for. If you want to investigate this way of packing further, check out some of the videos on the Internet. Rolling clothes for packing is practical; however, it is not everyone's preference and you can decide to fold or roll depending on the item, material and your liking. There is no right or wrong as long as you can see and access your items with ease.

You can make use of packing cubes/bags that you can then fit into your backpack. Packing cubes are all the rage these days as they make travelling with a suitcase a lot easier. You can, however, use them efficiently with a small backpack too. Please check the section "How to organise your bare minimum."

the "Bare Essentials" list below and start skimming off the items you accumulated. For EACH item, consider if you really need it. How many times have you used a similar thing in your daily life in the past year? Why do you think you might need it while travelling, if you hardly used it at home? Ask yourself if it is something you are likely to need on a regular basis or only as a one-off. In the latter case, please leave it at home. Also, make sure you can mix and match your tops and bottoms to come out with different outfits. If a top can only be worn with one bottom (and vice versa), it stays at home.

By using this method, you will find that you will need to pack less than half of what you initially thought.

What I have noticed is that it doesn't matter how many outfits you have in your bag, you always revert back to the few you feel comfortable in and forget the rest (much as we do at home, hence our closets are full of unused clothes). So I would urge you to go through the "Should I pack it?" diagram below for each item you plan to take with you.

Try to pack outfits that are loose fitting, of natural fibre, easy to wash and quick to dry. Much as you might look the part in spandex and tight-fitting gear, you will not be

TIPS ON PACKING

How do you learn what you need to pack? Three ways really:

1. Travel, return home and analyse what you used out of everything you took with you. Next time, make sure you only pack what you actually used.

2. Use other people's experience. Ask what lightweight packers take with them. Look at them. Are they dirty and smelly and look like they never changed their clothes or are they clean and just wear the same clothes every few days? If the latter, then you can definitely learn from them.

3. A mixture of the two above.

Packing does not have to be daunting and can be tackled rather quickly. I would, however, suggest not to pack too long in advance. If you do, you might forget what you have already stuffed in your bag and be tempted to just add to it inconsiderately. By all means, plan in advance, but do not pack. Lay out all the things you want to take with you and leave them there for a few days. Go through

What follows is a general guide for packing a light and efficient backpack for a trip to moderate-to-hot countries by an average size person not requiring any specific medical supplies.

Supplies

Please know that, unless you go directly to a deserted island or the middle of the jungle, you will definitely find shops all over the world where you can buy all your essentials, and you DO NOT need to carry them from home or stock up for the whole duration of the trip.

Shampoos, soaps, toothpaste, toothbrushes, shower gel, pain relief tablets, conditioner, sanitary towels, moisturising creams, sun creams, mosquito repellents, bandages, plasters, antiseptic creams, diarrhoea tablets, hand sanitisers, toilet paper, tissues, washing powder, flip-flops and many other items are sold all over the world, even in small towns and villages. You do not need to carry your stash from home.

For you lady travellers, I would say however that if you are used to tampons, those are harder to find, so if you really cannot see yourself go through a few periods without them, then stock up. I would argue, however, that for the sake of light luggage, you could forsake tampons for a few months. Or why not try a menstrual cups, sponges or reusable cloth pads instead? Cheaper and great for the environment.

Just make sure you do not jeopardise your health for the sake of not carrying the weight of your medicine.

Special requirements

There are also specific requirements that need to be taken into consideration. If any of the items of clothing you normally wear are made on purpose for you or are very difficult to find on the open market, you need to make sure you have them with you from the outset. For example, if you are a very large person, you need to keep in mind that sizes in Asia are different and you will be challenged to find anything that fits you, so plan accordingly. If, for example, you wear very large footwear or reinforced underwear, you will need to bring enough of them, as you will not be able to find them easily on your trip.

Camping

This guide is not intended for those of you who expect to camp as there are plenty more considerations there and I am not an expert on tents and required accessories. But please follow the same basic principles. If you are not sure you really need something, do not bring it, especially if you know you can buy it on-site if you really cannot live without it.

to tropical countries. You will definitely need to pack thermal clothes, jackets and jumpers as well as the right foot-wear. These kinds of trips are very specific, and I would not want to comment on the necessary requirements for a vacation to below-zero temperatures.

Likewise, if you are travelling to places with very different climates, you will need to cater to all of them accordingly.
One thing I would suggest, however, if your clothing is bulky, invest in compression bags which eliminate the air from your garments making them a lot less space consuming.

Health

If your health requires you to take specific medicines on a regular basis or you have life-threatening allergies, then you absolutely need to make sure that you have a sufficient supply of your medication to last you the whole trip. As an alternative, you could try to find out how to obtain your medicine in the countries you will be visiting. Although this is a perfectly viable solution, you need to be completely sure that your medication will be available and that you can easily get your hands on it in the country you select. This kind of research is entirely your responsibility, and I will not advocate either way.

CONSIDERATIONS

Your destination, health issues and specific requirements need to be considered when packing, but the length of your trip is irrelevant. You do not need to pack more because you will be away for a long period. You can just wash your clothes and use them over and over again. Or use, donate and buy a new item.

If you go travelling for two weeks, you might want to have enough to wear a different outfit each day of the week and therefore use the same outfit twice during the whole trip. If you go for ten weeks, you just need to wear it ten times. You will still carry seven outfits. When travelling, nobody notices or cares if you are wearing the same things repeatedly as long as you do not smell.

Destination

This guide is based on months-long trips to moderate-to-hot countries, where the temperature would not drop below 15 degrees Celsius at night and might go up well above the 25 degrees during the day. However, most of the advice and considerations apply to any trip.

If you pack to go to the Himalayas in winter, your luggage will look very different than if you are travelling

6. Mobility. A light bag means walking a few blocks is not a problem, you don't need an elevator or escalator.

7. Safety. Travelling with heavy luggage makes you more of a target for ill-intentioned individuals. You give the idea that you must be carrying value around with you. You will also find it much harder to get away in awkward situations.

The more stuff you have, the more stress you experience. Travelling with light luggage puts you in control of your experiences and helps you ensure that your trip is one to remember for all the right reasons.

3. Comfort. Carrying a heavy bag on and off public transport is uncomfortable at best and painful at worst. Have you tried getting on a crowded local bus with a 70 litres backpack? Or sitting with it on your lap for 5 hours? Not the best situation to be in.

4. Speed. If you are trying to get to your destination as quickly as possible, you do not want to have to wait for your luggage to eventually arrive on the carousel at the airport. You want to just clear passport control and be off on your new adventure (or to your hostel for a well-deserved rest).

5. Luggage security. If your luggage cannot be stored inside the bus/van, it will have to be put in the boot, on top of the vehicle, or somewhere outside the passengers' cabin and out of your sight… how safe is that? Are you sure you will find it once you reach your destination? And if it is lost. How much will this set you back in money and time, not to mention the loss of irreplaceable personal mementoes?

WHY TRAVEL LIGHT?

Carrying around heavy luggage has several disadvantages. Here are some of them:

1. Damage to your health. Carrying 15 Kg on your back is not healthy, and it can cause you problems. Do you really want to find a chiropractor miles away from home? Do you want to pay extortionate medical expenses? Do you want to delay your next move? All because you can't reduce the weight of your backpack?

2. Cost. Many airlines these days charge additional costs for luggage. Some of these costs are a lot higher than the price of the ticket itself. On the other hand, carry-on luggage is free, and the allowance varies between 5 and 10 Kg. If you make sure your backpack is the right size and within the weight limit for hand luggage, you will be saving yourself considerable travel costs and have a much wider choice of flights without incurring extra fees.

Being a minimalist by nature, I know I take shedding the unnecessary to extremes, but this trait has always served me very well. You can always adapt my extremism to your more moderate views, but the principles shared here will still be valid.

We generally travel well-known routes, and despite our beliefs that some of the countries we visit are very different from ours, my experience has shown me that the whole world is pretty similar and basic needs are met in very similar ways. You will find most of what you need in local shops, rest assured.

One thing I would urge you never to leave behind is **travel insurance**. Please make sure you are adequately covered for your trip. Read the small print and ensure all the activities you are planning on doing, and location you are planning on visiting are included, and the length of your trip is acceptable. A small saving on insurance can cause you unthinkable headaches. And there is absolutely no weight to it ;) Save the policy number and the emergency phone numbers in your phone for easy access.

and it is useless, you end up carrying it with you for months.

Travelling with valuable items is also stressful and takes away from the joy and excitement of travel. My advice is to pack what you can afford to lose. If you bring items that have a monetary or sentimental value (or both), you will spend most of your time worrying about them getting lost, stolen or broken. Don't do this to yourself. Bring a cheaper version of the same item. For example, your Ray Bans sunglasses might be your pride and joy, but do you really want to worry about them while you are on the road?

What is a "nice-to-have" while we are at home can easily be shed while travelling. We can pamper ourselves with niceties when we don't have to carry things on our backs, but we can still function without them when travelling. For example, a sponge, loafer or wash cloth might be very nice to have while in the shower at home, but it is unpractical –bulky and slow to dry -while you travel. By cutting right down on your "nice-to-haves," you might not have all your creature comforts while on the road, but the experiences will definitely be worth it.

My absolute favourites are tropical countries, so this is where I will share my experience on how to pack lightly. For cold countries, please adapt the general principles you will find in this guide, but make sure you pack according to the temperatures you will encounter.

One thing I have seen over and over again is backpackers buried under enormous baggage. It is so typical to see travellers with an overfilled 70 litre backpack on their back, a smaller (but heavy) pack strapped to the front, a waist bag and possibly a couple of other bags and a guitar. Maybe they will never ever be caught short of anything, but in the meantime, they have to drag all these belongings around the world.

On several occasions, I have had conversations with fellow globetrotters, and they all confirmed that most of their precious luggage was made up of things they had never used, had never even taken out of the backpack once.

It is much more difficult to abandon something you brought from home than buy something you discover you need once you are travelling. Subconsciously, you find it hard to discard an item you had when you were at home, so even if it has no monetary or sentimental value

INTRODUCTION

Not all who wander are lost.

J. R. R. Tolkien

Over the years, I have had the good fortune to travel extensively, both for work and pleasure and, although I still have many countries on my bucket list, so far I have been honoured to visit more than 40 countries on 5 different continents and the incredible luck to live in 3 of them, one of which was a tropical island. From Australia to Argentina, from Brazil to India, Costa Rica to Indonesia, France to South Africa, Romania to Morocco, Russia to the Caribbean, Turkey to Sri Lanka and plenty between. Each journey, taught me to trim and remould my luggage to ensure that I can travel at length without being hindered by heavy bags, still having enough to be comfortable. The result? A baggage (☺) of experience I want to share with you to make your luggage as comfortable, light and practical as mine.

THE LIGHT-PACKER GUIDE

FOREWORD

Want to travel the world but not be burdened by heavy luggage? Don't know what to pack and think you'll need your kitchen sink?

There are ways to travel as light as for a day trip and still have everything you need on the other side of the world. Spend more time exploring and less packing and unpacking. Less, in this case, really is more.

Follow me in this journey through what we really need and what we can easily do without. In this guide I share the what, the why and the how of light packing.

- Denim 49
- Neck pillow 49
- Books 50
- Guide books 50
- Maps 51
- Laptops 51
- Professional cameras 52
- Mosquito repellent 53
- Sun-cream 53
- Tools 54
- Shaving 54
- Jewellery 55
- Musical instruments 55
- Make-up 56
- Laundry 56
- Exercise 57

THE LIST 59
- List for women 60
- List for men 62

THE WHYS AND WHY NOTS 39

Smartphone 39

Sim Cards 40

Credit cards 40

Walking shoes 41

Sandals 42

Hat 42

Diary 42

Torch 43

Swimwear 43

Skirts 44

Shorts 44

Flip-flop socks 45

Pyjama 45

Sarong/Pareo 45

Small day bag 46

Pack away backpack/bag 46

Liquids 46

Earphones 47

Personal reusable straws 47

Collapsible reusable water bottle 47

Small combination padlock 49

Table of Contents

FOREWORD 1

INTRODUCTION 3

WHY TRAVEL LIGHT? 7

CONSIDERATIONS 11

    Destination 11

    Health 12

    Special requirements 13

    Camping 13

    Supplies 14

TIPS ON PACKING 17

SHOULD I PACK IT? 23

THE BACKPACK 25

THE BARE MINIMUM 29

    A.   Essentials 29

    B.   Clothes 30

        For women 30

        For men 31

    C.   Other Items 32

    D.   Toiletries etc. 33

    E.   Buy on site when you arrive 34

    How to organise your bare minimum 37